NICK CANLEY

MAKING WEBSITES WIN

The Ultimate Guide to Boosting Traffic to Your Website, Learn About Content Marketing SEO and Other Effective Marketing Techniques to Ensure Traffic For Your Website

Descrierea CIP a Bibliotecii Naționale a României
NICK CANLEY
    MAKING WEBSITES WIN. The Ultimate Guide to
Boosting Traffic to Your Website, Learn About Content
Marketing SEO and Other Effective Marketing Techniques to
Ensure Traffic For Your Website / Nick Canley. – Bucharest:
Editura My Ebook, 2020
    ISBN

NICK CANLEY

MAKING WEBSITES WIN

The Ultimate Guide to Boosting Traffic to Your Website, Learn About Content Marketing SEO and Other Effective Marketing Techniques to Ensure Traffic For Your Website

My Ebook Publishing House
Bucharest, 2020

TABLE OF CONTENTS

CHAPTER 1

INTRODUCTION

There was a time when running a successful online business or making passive income was new and unheard of. There was a time when it took a courageous and pioneering spirit to make a full time living from a blog.

But that's changed. Stories of people becoming *extremely* successful through social media and running a website are now commonplace. It's been happening for decades.

And yet it's *still* something that a lot of people don't understand and aren't taking advantage of.

This is a HUGE missed opportunity. What's the key ingredient here? TRAFFIC. That is a high **volume** of traffic.

And highly **targeted** traffic.

This isn't just for entrepreneurs and bloggers either. If you run a business with any kind of online component, then traffic is the key to making sales. Traffic is the lifeblood of any online business.

Let's say that you have an online store and you're currently using that sells hats. Right now, you get around 500 visitors to your site a day, which leads to 2-3 sales, or about $40-60 profit. It's a small side project that is earning you a bit of cash doing something you enjoy.

With the right strategies, you could easily increase your visitors to a similar 150,000 daily within a year or two. Those 2-3 sales now become 60-90 sales.

And what if you leverage that success to start selling other products? To build a successful YouTube channel or Instagram account?

The sky is the limit.

Even for a local business such as a restaurant, increasing your traffic has the potential to massively increase sales.

Right now let's say you get 100 orders every night, which is largely due to word of mouth. But what if your website was the first one to come up on Google? What if people could order through your site with a few clicks?

What if you had a thriving Facebook page or group and a strong community?

You could *easily* increase the number of orders you get. None of this is easy, but none of it is hard either.

This book will serve as your guide. It will show you some of the most effective ways and methods of generating traffic to your website.

CHAPTER 2

CONTENT MARKETING

If you've been moving in digital marketing circles for a while, you've probably heard it said that 'content is king'.

And it's not without reason, because when done right content marketing is a mind-blowing powerful strategy.

How powerful? Well, **research** has shown that it can cost up to 62% less than traditional marketing and generate about three times as many leads.

If you want to start driving more traffic to your website, then there is one *single* thing that you need to be doing. This indisputable, critical aspect of your marketing is non-negotiable and has the biggest potential for increasing your viewers, your authority, and your engagement.

That is to apply content marketing.

What is Content Marketing?

Content marketing is about using media such as blogs, newsletters, social posts, videos and infographics to draw customers towards you. How? By providing value upfront.

> *Content marketing flips the script on traditional marketing. Instead of roaring at your audience through a megaphone, content marketing transforms your business into a powerful magnet that pulls customers to your doorstep.*

The reason this is so crucial is simple: the internet is *built* on content. Most of the time you spend online will likely be either reading or watching videos, both of which are examples of *content consumption.*

To find that content, you probably searched for a phrase or term in Google, and Google will then have matched your query to content that it had indexed.

Why You Need to Implement Content Marketing

When you add high-quality content to your website on a regular basis, you achieve a number of things:

- You provide free value

- You demonstrate your knowledge and expertise in your niche and become an expert

- You increase brand awareness and trust exponentially

- You provide Google with a means of understanding what your site is about

- You create more pages for your site, each of which can then act as a potential entry point to your site and your brand

- You gain a commodity that you can share on social media

- You increase the likelihood of people who enjoy your content sharing it with other people: thereby giving you free links and free exposure.

How To Write an Engaging Blog Post

One of the key ingredients to your success then is to write a high quantity of articles. The more you write, the more opportunity you create to be discovered. The more questions you can answer, and the more people you can engage with.

As a starting point, I recommend writing **at least one blog post a week**. This is far from ideal, though. Far preferable would be 3-4 posts per week, and potentially even a post a day.

What's arguably more important, though, is that you learn to write high- quality blog posts. If you get this wrong, then it doesn't matter how many you write!

Only a high-quality blog post will increase the likelihood of someone returning to your website, and only a high-quality blog post will increase the likelihood that your site will get shared.

So, what does the perfect blog post look like?

First and most important is that your post should not be derivative. This means you should not be sharing content for the sake of it. Every single post needs to have something unique to say.

Let's consider two approaches to fitness.

One blog post on fitness is an exclusive interview with the elusive and extremely in-demand Ido Portal. His is a completely unique approach to training and one that has set the social media world on fire for several years now (he's a real guy, look him up!).

The other is an article called "5 Exercises for Six Pack Abs." Which will perform better?

The way I've phrased this question means that it may be obvious. But for many, it is not. In fact, many articles and gurus will claim that the latter is superior.

On the face of it, the second title looks like a goldmine. Everyone wants six- pack abs. This is an extremely high-volume keyword/keyphrase (meaning people search for it a lot), and it has a great list format.

But here's the problem: most of us have read *thousands* of articles just like it! This is an issue because it means that no one is going to be that excited by it.

Which article would you be more likely to want to click?

Even if it comes up at the top of the SERPs (Search Engine Results Pages), an article still needs to entice the visitor to click on it because they want to read it!

Then there's the issue of this content being so competitive. With thousands of similar articles, how will you make sure yours gets to the top of Google?

On the other hand, the interview is unique content that has a built-in following. People who love Ido Portal are almost guaranteed to like and share this post, especially if you can get it to the right places by sharing it on social media.

Anyone who *hasn't* heard of him might have their interest piqued. A *new* approach to fitness? Really? What is a "movement first" attitude anyway?

Then there are the long-tail keywords. You might not easily be able to rank for a top keyword with this post, but people will find you when they search for related terms. These include such things as:

- Movement culture
- Just move
- Ido Portal
- Ido Portal interview

These can get you a decent number of *targeted* visitors (meaning they are visitors that will find your content interesting and be likely to buy from you). They can also bring you an increasing number of visitors as these terms *grow*.

Post lots of content like this – long-form and at least 800 words – and then make an effort to really share it. Promote each blog post like you would promote an entirely new product!

Do all this, and you'll find that your content helps to gradually increase in- roads to your site, while at the same time building up your reputation, exposure, and influence.

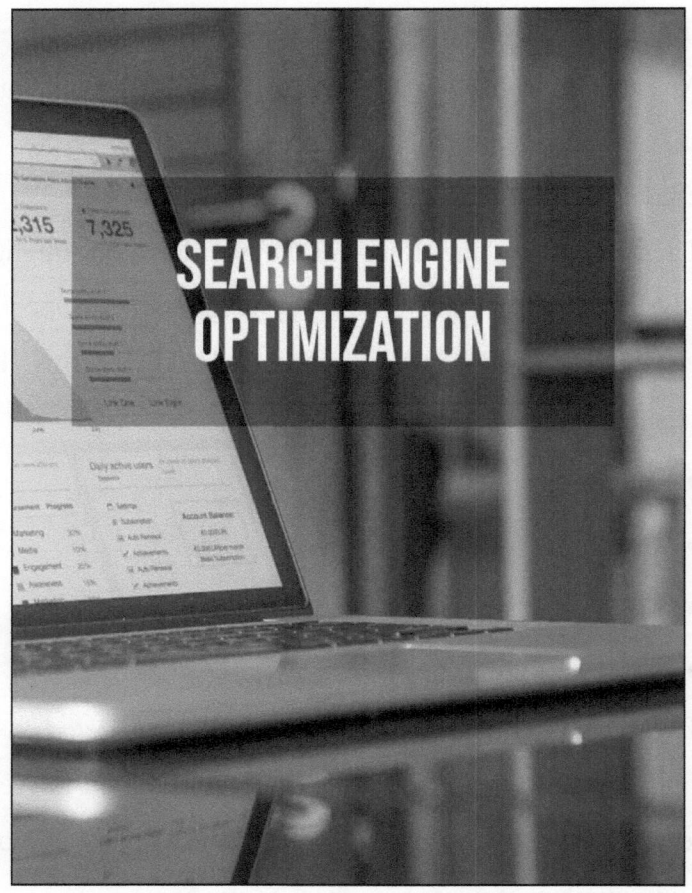

CHAPTER 3

SEO

The other piece of the puzzle when it comes to high-quality content is SEO.

The chances are that you know what SEO is. SEO is a series of techniques that can be used to get a website to reach the top of Google. This stands for "Search Engine Optimization."

This is a topic that has been written about ad nauseam. The problem is that many of these blog posts, articles, and videos only serve to muddy the waters and create more confusion regarding precisely what SEO is all about.

It's certainly true that SEO is changing all the time, and that it is multifaceted. This can make it difficult to know where to focus your efforts.

But ultimately, there are two crucial ingredients for effective SEO and one important rule that binds them together.

The ingredients are:

- Keywords

- Links

And the important rule is:

- Provide value

Keywords

Google works by finding content and adding it to a huge database (index) where it keeps every single one of its links. When somebody searches for a phrase, Google then refers to that database in order to retrieve the most relevant, high-quality webpage to attempt to answer the question.

Keywords are what Google uses to recognize the content of a webpage and thereby to know who to show it to. We want our website to be shown to as many people as possible, and so we should look for keywords that a lot of people are searching for. More often than not, this will mean looking for popular phrases and things that are currently trending.

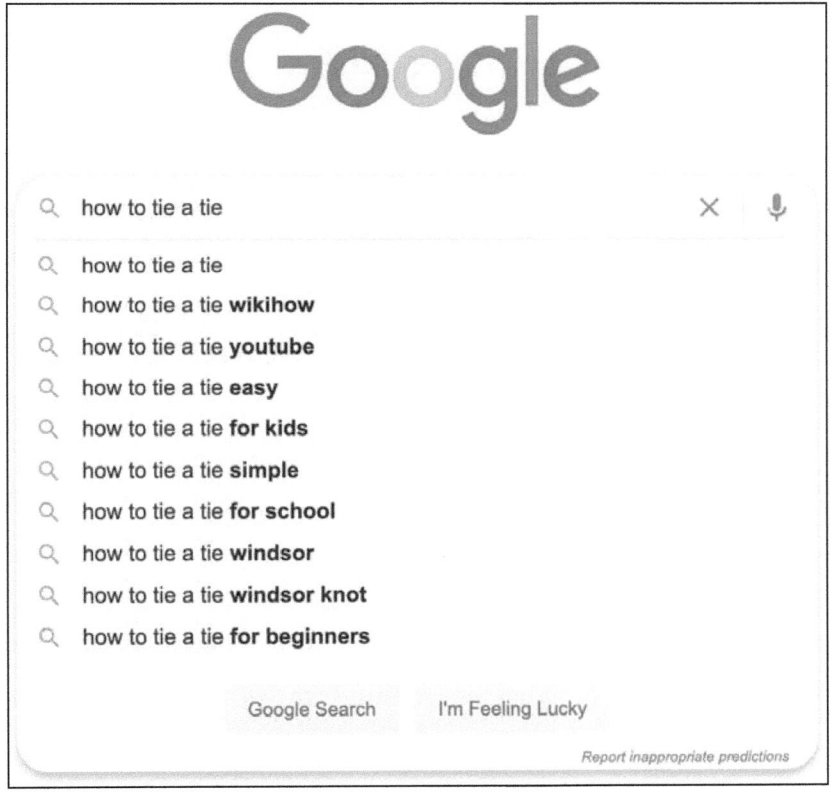

To show Google that our content is highly relevant to that keyword, we then need to lace our website with those keywords as much as possible.

One way to do this is by repeating the phrase throughout our content. We don't want to overdo this though, or it will look like we're trying to spam the system.

> *The best way to include keywords in content is to try and make the keyword often appear, while simultaneously avoiding doing too much.*
> *The best advice is to follow a rule of 0.5-2% density. That means that you should include a keyword once every 50-200 words. Be guided by what feels natural: if it is going to stand out to the reader as forced, then leave it out.*
> *It is far better to "underdo" your SEO than it is to overdo it!*

LSI (Latent Semantic Indexing)

Moreover, you should aim to use related terms and synonyms. This is what is referred to as "latent semantic indexing" or LSI. This is how Google looks for the kinds of increased use of specific phrases that would *naturally* occur in a post about a given subject. It's important for you to understand the subject you are writing about well so that you can naturally include all of the related terms and phrases that you would normally when writing in that niche!

Note: This is also how you go about covering new ground when writing blog posts. We mentioned before how important it was to avoid writing derivative and "overplayed" content. The only way you can go about doing this is to make sure that the content you write is in a topic that you understand and you are passionate about.

9 Other Elements to Optimize For Search Engines

There are also some particular areas in a post that benefit particularly from the use of keywords. These are:

1. The title
2. The first paragraph
3. Headers throughout the text
4. The last paragraph

You should also aim to use the keyphrases in the code and file names of your website. Useful ways to include this include:

5. Alt tags for images
6. Meta description
7. SEO title
8. File names for images
9. The slug of your web page

Should You Only Target One Keyword or Keyphrase?

It's okay to target more than one keyword, and in fact, a good strategy is to have one "primary" keyword along with a couple of secondary options.

If you can do all this as much as possible without making it stand out obviously to the reader, then you will have effectively laced your content with keywords!

If you're not sure of how to do this and you are using WordPress to run your website, then you can always try using a powerful tool called YoastSEO (**https://yoast.com/wordpress/plugins/seo**).

This plugin will look at the content of your blog posts, and it will highlight areas where your SEO could be better: by using more search terms in your opening and closing paragraphs for example, or by using keywords in your headers.

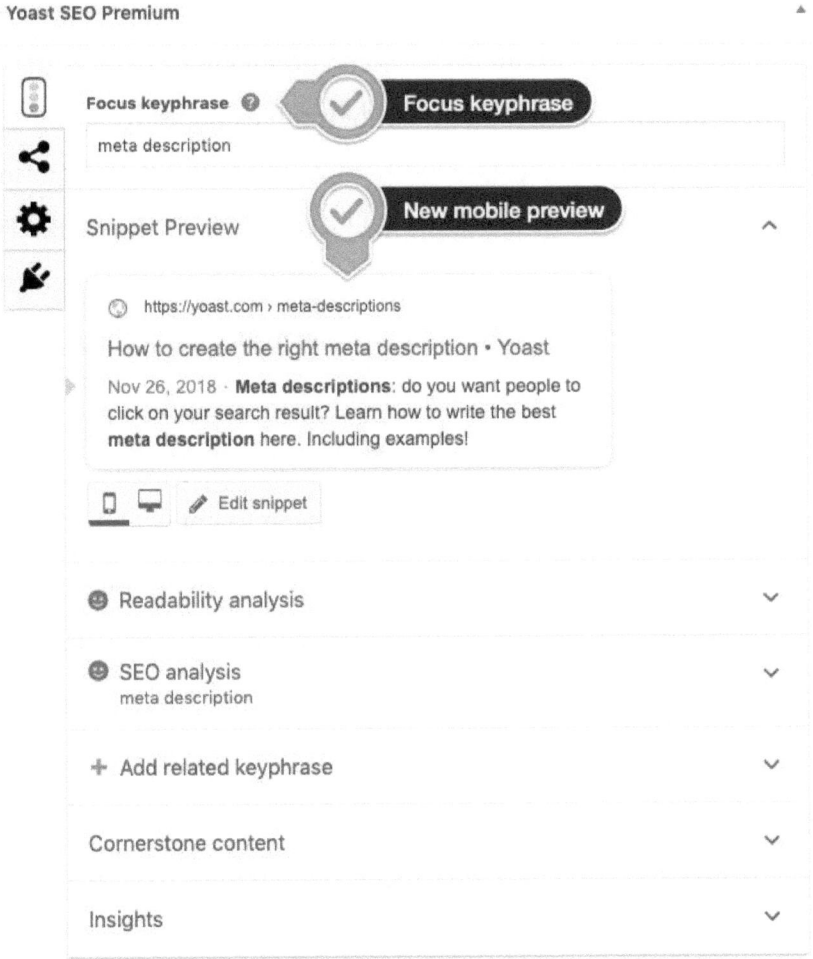

Source: Yoast

When using YoastSEO, you shouldn't expect to reach a "green status" every single time. Some articles will have a great social media value, but won't lend themselves naturally to SEO. Other articles will have keywords that are difficult to fit into your content. The aim is simply to be aware of these methods and to tick all the boxes *as often as possible*. This is the mindset to have when performing SEO for your website and webpages.

3 Types of Keywords You Need to Know About

There are 3 types of keyword you need to know about:

- Short Keywords - broad concepts, e.g. swimming

- Medium Keywords - narrowed down concept, e.g. swimming goggles

- Long-tail Keywords - more specific again, e.g. swimming goggles for triathlon

Typically, short keywords are the hardest to rank for, followed by medium and then long-tail. This is because there's less competition for long-tail keywords. So, we'll be aiming mainly to target longer-tail keywords with 2-4 words.

How to Find Keywords Using The Google Keyword Planner Tool

Of course, there is one more step when it comes to building an effective SEO campaign using keywords... and that is to actually *find* the right keywords in the first place. How do you know what people are searching for?

To do this, you can use Google's Keyword Planner Tool.

Step 1. Go to **https://ads.google.com/home/tools/keyword-planner/**

Step 2. Sign in to your Google account.

Step 3. Select the option that says **Discover new keywords**.

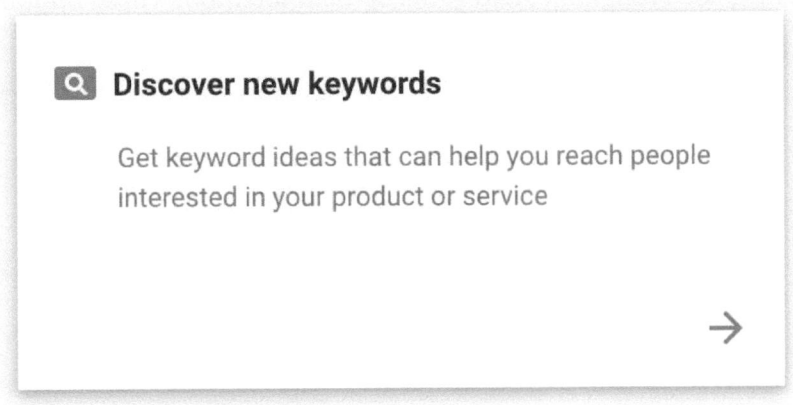

This option will search not only for a keyword or keyphrase you enter, but Google will also show related keywords, too.

Step 4. Enter a keyword.

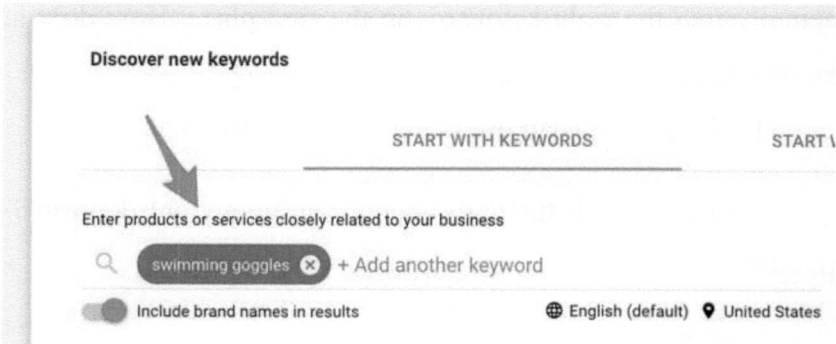

Step 5. Set your criteria. Choose whether to include *brand names*, set a *language*, and *geographical location*. These options may be useful if you are only targeting a specific country.

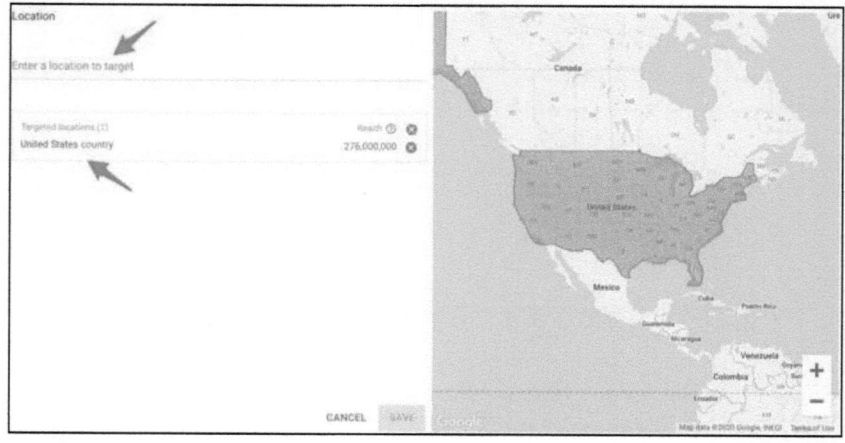

Step 6. Click **Get Results** once set.

Step 7. Browse through the keywords that Google has now presented you with.

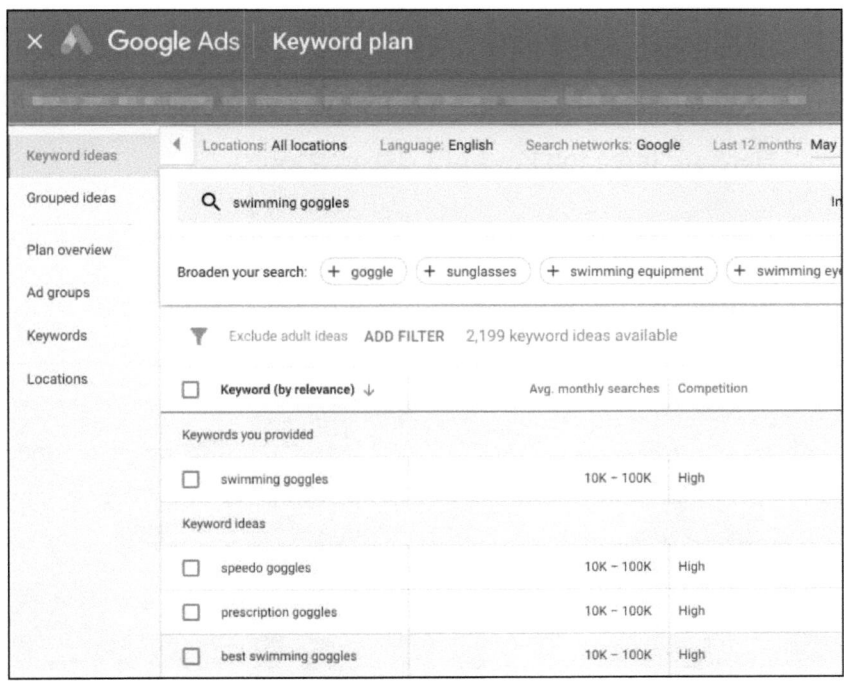

This tool is aimed at customers using Google Ads, but it can help you to get an idea of the volume of traffic looking for any given keyphrase.

The screenshot above shows the average monthly searches for "swimming googles" is 10K – 100K. That means this keyphrase gets searched 10,000 to 100,000 times each month.

Other Keyword Research Tools To Consider

Should you need more data, then you can pay for a third party tool – though these are typically quite expensive.

Here are three top keyword research tools:

KeywordTool.io
https://keywordtool.io/

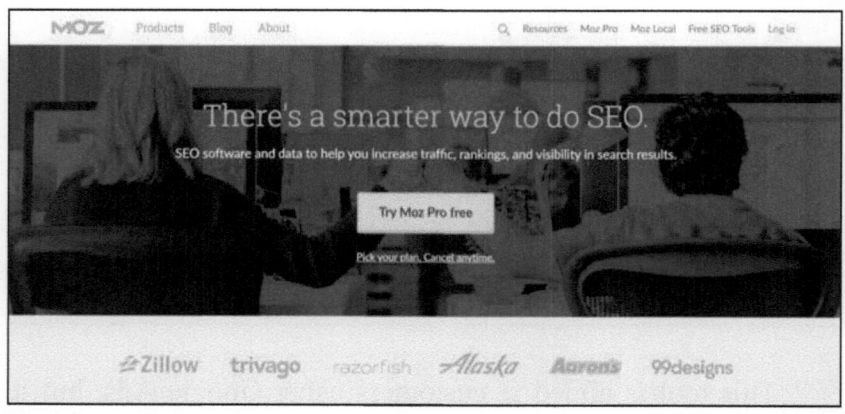

Moz
https://moz.com

SEMRush

https://www.semrush.com/

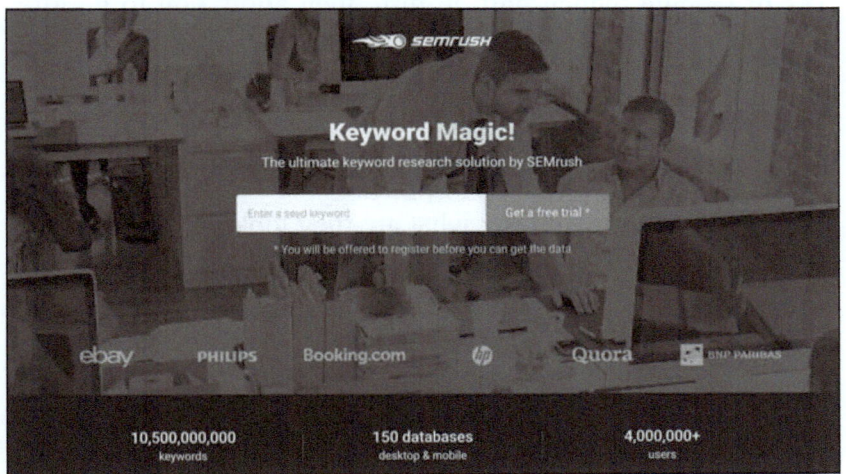

Which Keywords Should You Go For?

The aim is to look for keywords that have a **high volume of traffic, but not too much competition.**

As with most things, the more established your site is (meaning it has "domain age" as well as lots of backlinks and tons of content), the more easily you'll be able to go after the highest-ranking keywords. A great strategy then is to view this as a ladder. When starting out, go for the low- hanging fruit. Aim to get to the top of Google for those terms that are a little more obscure, but that could still get you a few hundred visitors per month.

This will then help you to establish yourself a little in the eyes of Google, which will, in turn, then allow you to go after slightly more popular links!

Another **extremely** important thing to consider is the matter of "intent." Intent refers to the intention of the person searching for the keyphrase: what are they looking for and why?

This is very important because it is what will ensure you attract the *right* people to your website. For instance, someone might phrase a term differently depending on whether they want to buy something or just ask about it.

"Hats online" AND "buy hats online" are probably keywords that suggest a person is looking to buy a hat. If you have a hat store, then this can be a great way to get people to your site!

But if you have an article that is all about hat style, then calling it "hats online" will likely mean you get the *wrong* type of person visiting your page. This can, in turn, mean that they leave that page very quickly, which in turn means your "bounce rate" will be high (meaning people leave your site before they have spent any time there). A high bounce rate significantly hurts your reputation in Google's eyes, and it means that Google will *stop recommending* your site when people search for related terms!

It's not just about what you can rank for then: it's about understanding your visitors and what they might be looking for.

Backlinks

Backlinks play three important roles in Google's systems. Firstly, they allow Google to find your content in the first place. Google trawls the web using programs called "spiders" or sometimes "robots." These programs work by following links to move from one website to another.

So by having as many backlinks to your website as possible, you make it easier for Google to find you and therefore put you in the index.

At the same time, Google looks at links as another way to know what your site is about. If your site has lots of links coming from sites about fitness, then it will assume that your site is *also* about fitness!

Finally, Google will look at links as testimony. Links suggest quality because people don't tend to share links to websites that they don't think are very good!

The more backlinks you have to your site, the more Google will consider your site to be important and valuable. Much MORE importantly, though, Google will also want to see that your links are coming from pages that it already trusts.

For instance, if you have a link from the BBC, Google will consider that to be *endlessly* more worthwhile than a link from a website that is full of spam.

Looking for links that Google is known to trust is perhaps the single best way to increase your chances of climbing the ranks. One way to do this is to look for links with .edu and .gov TLDs. Another option is to look for the sites that Google commonly features in the SERPs.

Finally, look at the top competition that you want to beat and then use a backlink checker that will show you the links point at *that* website. You can then try to get those same sites to link to you – as you know that they a) will give out links and b) can help you get to where you need to be!

The best way to get backlinks from other sites?

Guest post! That means writing a high-quality article for that website, then giving it to the website for free in exchange for a link that will point back to your website. This strategy has been used online for a long time, but it is still highly effective. Not only does this gain you a link back from a site in your niche that is high value, but it also helps you to build important relationships that can help you to succeed. You'll gain *direct traffic* from the recommendation that comes from being on a high-quality website.

One more tip? If you are going to succeed at guest posting (and SEO in general), then your website needs to be high quality. This is another way to keep bounce rates low, but it also ensures that bloggers in other niches will want to work with you.

Be honest with yourself: go and take a hard look at the very best/biggest blog/website in your niche. Can you honestly say that your website competes with that site in terms of presentation and content quality?

A top creator is *not* going to want to link to you if your site is covered in ads, or if it looks like it was built in the Geocities era (the early 00s, for those not familiar with their early websites!). You need to look the part if you're going to succeed. And this plays out in another way too.

Value

It's important to remember that Google serves the user. That is to say that Google is not interested in making life easier for blog owners. If your website provides valuable and useful information, then Google will want to share it with its visitors.

Why? Because if Google's visitors constantly find the high-quality content they are looking for – if they consistently have a good experience when searching on Google – then they will want to do it more often!

If Google's visitors find that the websites that get brought up are low quality, or that they don't contain the right information (mismatch between intent and content), then they will eventually *stop using Google*.

That's why Google looks at key factors such as the amount of time spent on your website when determining your potential ranking. It's why Google favors brands over sites that focus purely on keywords, and it's why Google is now strongly emphasizing the importance of a website that **loads quickly** and that **performs well on mobile**. If your website is not mobile-friendly, then fixing that limitation should be one of your *chief* concerns!

This is why Google is constantly changing its algorithm. The algorithm defines how Google searches for content, and thus bloggers and site owners are constantly trying to second guess it in order to unravel the secret formula to success. If only they can find out what Google is looking for, then they will be able to build successful web pages every single time!

Google doesn't make its algorithms public though, and so SEO optimizers are left to guess. They will then often come to conclusions such as "Google wants to see 3% density for keywords" or "Google wants you to collect as *many* links as humanly possible."

The problem is that Google will then invariably change the goalposts by altering its algorithm. Suddenly, collecting thousands of links without giving any regard to their quality is actually going to hurt your website's ranking! In fact, this precise thing happened once, and it led to many websites being completely removed from Google (this is called being "de-indexed.")

Historic algorithm changes like this have put huge companies out of business and devastated entire industries! And those people trying to optimize their websites had only been doing what other companies had *told* them to do for marketing purposes. They had only been doing what they *thought* Google wanted them to do!

Of course, this is a difficult subject. After all, this has seriously affected many people's lives – and Google's monopoly over search gives the company responsibility to businesses.

But at the same time, Google never *asked* those businesses to try and "game" the algorithm. The company never came out and stated that people should be building links on low-quality websites.

Those business owners that followed this approach simply missed the point: that Google serves the customer.

We can't predict future changes to the algorithm, but we can guarantee that Google is trying to serve the visitor first (while also taking care of its own needs, by ensuring people stay on its own pages for longer). As long as you focus on delivering high-quality content on a well-designed website, and as long as your content *answers* the questions posed in the search terms, then your goals will be aligned with Google's, and you should benefit from future changes.

Rich Snippets

One more aspect to consider for your marketing is the use of rich snippets. Rich snippets show a higher quantity of information from your website, often with a bulleted list, or an image.

These are used by Google to try and keep visitors on the SERPs for longer. Google ideally would love to cut out content creators altogether in order to retain that valuable traffic! Thus, Google's spiders can look for specific elements in your text and share those directly with visitors. These include things like dates and locations of events, as well as recipes, the answers to questions, and more.

Here is an example of what a rich snippet search result looks like:

✔ thebigmansworld.com › Desserts › Homemade Can ▾

Homemade Keto Chocolate Crunch Bars (Paleo, Vegan, Low ...

 Mar 29, 2018 - Ingredients. 1 1/2 cups chocolate chips of choice I used stevia sweetened **keto** friendly chocolate chips. 1 cup almond butter Can sub for any **nut** or seed butter of choice. 1/2 cup sticky sweetener of choice * See notes. 1/4 cup coconut oil. 3 cups **nuts** and seeds of choice almonds, cashews, pepitas etc.
★★★★★ Rating: 4.9 - 83 votes - 10 min. - Calories: 155

You will see extra information such as Rating, Votes, cooking time, and Calories:

✓ thebigmansworld.com › Desserts › Homemade Can ▾

Homemade Keto Chocolate Crunch Bars (Paleo, Vegan, Low ...

 Mar 29, 2018 - Ingredients. 1 1/2 cups chocolate chips of choice I used stevia sweetened **keto** friendly chocolate chips. 1 cup almond butter Can sub for any **nut** or seed butter of choice. 1/2 cup sticky sweetener of choice * See notes. 1/4 cup coconut oil. 3 cups **nuts** and seeds of choice almonds, cashews, pepitas etc.
★★★★★ Rating: 4.9 - 83 votes - 10 min. - Calories: 155

By using a special "Schema" markup, you can communicate key elements to Google and ensure that Google chooses *your* page to highlight in the SERPs. This might lose you some traffic – seeing as people are now getting their cooking instructions without having to visit your page! But you will lose far *less* traffic than you would if another brand were chosen instead of yours. Moreover, this will help you to improve brand awareness and will lead to more visitors in the long term.

Not sure how to implement schema markups? Then visit Schema.org for the full documentation. Alternatively, there are plugins for WordPress that can help you with the process. This is one of the key features of modern SEO, so don't get left behind!

SOCIAL MEDIA MARKETING

CHAPTER 4

SOCIAL MEDIA MARKETING

Social media for marketing is a concept that is hugely misunderstood by the vast majority of big brands trying to bring more traffic to their websites.

You see this all the time. Take a look at many of the brands on Facebook or Twitter, and you'll see them repeating the same mistakes. Primarily, that means posting *over and over again* about the same promotional nonsense, without giving any thought to strategy or value.

These posts look like this:

- Why not sign up to our mailing list today to find out more about our business?

- Did you know that our CRM system was rated the top new software product last year?

- Sign up now for 20% off of our latest software package!

- Is your business doing everything it can to maximize efficiency?

And on and on!

Answer this: would you consider following a social media account that *only* published these types of comments?

The answer for us is no, and the reason is obvious: there is no value being provided here!

What's more, is that these messages will be sporadic and random and with no real goal in mind. Then the owner of the business wonders why they don't see the huge numbers they feel they deserve for their efforts!

There are four key things you need to understand if you are going to successfully use social media to drive traffic:

- Value
- Community
- Integration
- Consistency

Value

This should be obvious. If you want people to follow you on *any* platform, then you need to give them a good reason to do so. That means that you need to be able to offer some kind of value for their time, their effort, and their contact details.

In the case of social media, there are a few ways you can do this.

On Instagram, the best fitness brands *don't* just post random pictures of themselves topless. Instead, they combine these pictures with useful insights and information that might help someone reading to improve their own training and results.

Likewise, if you run a business brand, you can provide useful money- making tips. If you run a blog about makeup, you should provide tips that can help someone create a better look.

What's key to understand here is that this is not just true for independent blogs. Many businesses assume that providing tips is "unprofessional" and should be left to the influencers. They instead want to post *business stuff*.

You can be as professional as you like though. If no one wants to read what you have to say, then you aren't going to get any followers! Anyone who *does* follow will leave.

Why would you want to see what amounts to advertising all over your home feed?

Another challenge for businesses is finding a way to offer value in what might be a very dull niche. For example, if you offer life insurance, then what could you offer to your readers that might be relevant? Makeup tips are hardly applicable here!

In this case, it is perfectly acceptable to think a little outside the box: to think about what you can offer that will provide value for the target audience.

Someone looking for life insurance is likely to be:

- An adult

- Married with children

- A homeowner

- Health-conscious and money conscious

Therefore, you might provide regular tips for families: ideas for days out, ways to stay healthy, ways to save money. These are things that benefit the target audience while being tangentially relevant to the services or products you are offering.

If 90% of your posts provide genuine value on this subject matter, then the other 10% can be used to promote your service and to drive sales. This works in *any* niche, as long as you are consistent.

Selling the Dream

There's another, less tangible way that you can deliver value to your audience through social media too. That is to focus on inspiring your audience. This is something that Instagram, in particular, is very well-known for.

The idea is simple: people follow brands because they want to feel inspired and motivated. For example, you might follow a fitness brand because you are inspired by images of people going for long runs or training hard at the gym. These images sell a "dream" and a value proposition: they make the viewer think about how they might feel if they were to achieve a similar level of fitness.

Meanwhile, brands about making money online might post images of themselves working hard at a computer through the night. Or they might post images of them giving talks in front of thousands of people, or looking out of highrise buildings wearing sharp suits.

Think about the "dream" that your business is selling and show this through your social media. If you can do this, then you will bring a large audience on board that will not only loyally follow your content, but also be more likely to visit your website – and buy any products you sell or recommend.

Community

Another more nebulous subject that is nevertheless extremely important when it comes to promoting your brand on social media is the idea of community.

Too many companies believe that social media is essentially a foghorn: a tool that they can use to shout loudly and reach a loud audience with a marketing message.

But social media is much more than that. In fact, *primarily,* social media is a communication tool! Understanding this is what will allow you to tap into its full power.

When you post something to social media, it's very important that you also engage with the audience who comment on it. Likewise, you should actively participate in other discussions or comment on other images.

This helps your audience to feel as though they know you, which once again makes them far more loyal to your business. You'll find they are then more likely to:

- Share your content
- Visit your website multiple times
- Engage with future posts

Think about it this way: if you were to ask your friends to share your links, chances are they would go above and beyond the call of duty to do so.

Imagine if you can create a legion of followers with that same sense of duty to you!

A great strategy is to create a Facebook group. This will allow you to develop a particularly loyal audience that you can almost guarantee will visit your site for every new post.

Integration

I also mentioned the importance of having a strategy. That means knowing *how* your social media is going to fit into a broader plan to promote your business and drive traffic to a website.

What's the point of developing fantastic social media presence if you're not going to do anything with it? This is another typical mistake for many businesses.

The answer is to use each of your "platforms" to promote each of your *other* platforms. You can do this in a few ways:

- Reminding people to follow you on social media in your content

- Reminding people to visit your website from your social media posts

- Sharing (high value) content from your website to your social media accounts

- Including social sharing buttons on your website so that people can easily share your post

- Re-sharing old posts on social media – you don't only have to post new content!

- Including social links on your homepage

- Even including a feed right on your website – so that people who visit can easily see that they can follow you through other places too

Consistency

Finally, none of this will work unless you are consistent. If your social media accounts are like ghost towns for months on end, then you won't see them grow! Not only does this play badly with the algorithms, but it also looks unprofessional!

Consistency means posting regularly, but it also means having consistent messaging, branding, and quality. That means your content should be on as many platforms as possible, but it also means that you should have a consistent brand and style across all of those platforms. Your logo and URL should be recognizable between Facebook, Instagram, and Twitter!

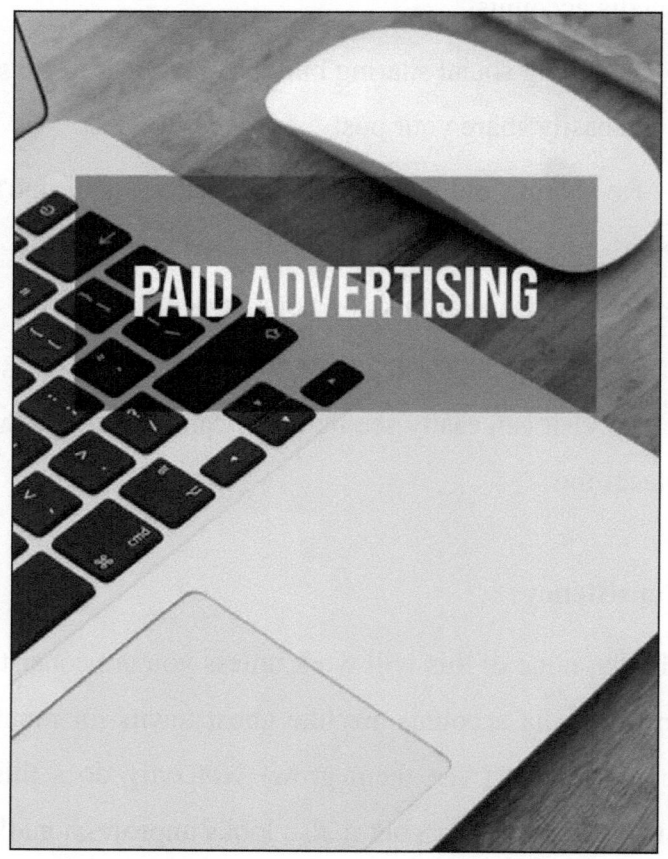

CHAPTER 5

PAID ADVERTISING

While all of this can make a big difference, we are so far missing out on one major strategy for generating traffic for a website: paid advertising.

If you want to get eyeballs on your website, then paying for ads is one of *the* most effective strategies.

That's because paid ads guarantee you a top spot for a particular keyword, or guarantee that you will get targeted exposure to the right people via social media.

Facebook Ads and Google Ads

There are two major forms of paid advertising that are popular on the web for smaller businesses with modest budgets. These are:

- Google Ads
- Facebook Ads

Google Ads is particularly effective as it will help you to get your links to the very top of Google. These are the ads that show above the "organic results" as sponsored links. This places them in a prominent place, and it means that you can target the same intent as you might do with SEO.

In other words, you can show your ads to someone who has searched for how to *buy* the product that you sell! Or that has searched for the kind of information you *specifically* provide. This is extremely valuable.

Google Ads also have the benefit of letting you test different search terms to see, which might bring the most traffic. You can this way ensure that a particular search term will be worth chasing after with SEO strategies.

Facebook Ads work slightly differently by showing ads on the home feeds of Facebook users. This time, you will target the position of your ad based on the interests and details of the user. As users, we give an awful lot of information to Facebook:

- Age

- Sex

- Location

- Interests

- Relationship status

- Hobbies

- Social network

- Job title

- Potentially even income!

This means that if you run a website selling wedding dresses, then you can use Facebook to show ads to:

- Women

- With high disposable income

- Who are local

- Who are engaged

PPC Explained

What makes both Ads and Facebook Ads particularly powerful, though, is that these are both forms of PPC advertising. PPC stands for "Pay Per Click", and it essentially means that the advertiser *only pays* if someone clicks on the ad.

Therefore, if your ad is unsuccessful in getting attention, it won't cost you anything! If your ad is shown and no one clicks on it, you'll gain brand exposure completely free!

What's more, is that this system allows you to calculate exactly how much you are willing to pay for each of your visitors, which in turn can guarantee a profit.

Pay per click advertising works using a bidding system. This means that you choose the *maximum* amount that you are willing to pay for your ad. When a relevant slot comes up for your ad to show, you will then enter into a bidding war with any other advertisers that are trying to advertise in the same spot. The advertiser with the highest maximum bid will be the one that wins, and you'll only pay the amount necessary to get the position.

That means that a lot of the time, you actually won't need to pay the full amount you have pledged: you might pay just 10 cents! It also means that the more competitive a keyword is, the more you will need to pay.

But what this *also* means is that you can now calculate the maximum amount you pay for each visitor. You can then measure this against your CLV (Customer Lifetime Value), and that way find out precisely how much you are profiting from your campaign.

For example, if you sell an eBook for $50 and you have a conversion rate of 2%, that means that you will earn $100 for every 100 visitors (this is just hypothetical – that would be an extremely high conversion rate in reality).

Now if you have a maximum bid of anything under $1, that should almost *guarantee profit* as long as the ads run for long enough!

Video Ads

Another extremely powerful tool that is under-utilized by a lot of marketers is video. Video ads shown on YouTube (before videos) and Instagram (in the feed) have a huge potential to make a massive impact on your visitors. That's because these videos have the potential to make a massive impact that makes a strong impression for your brand.

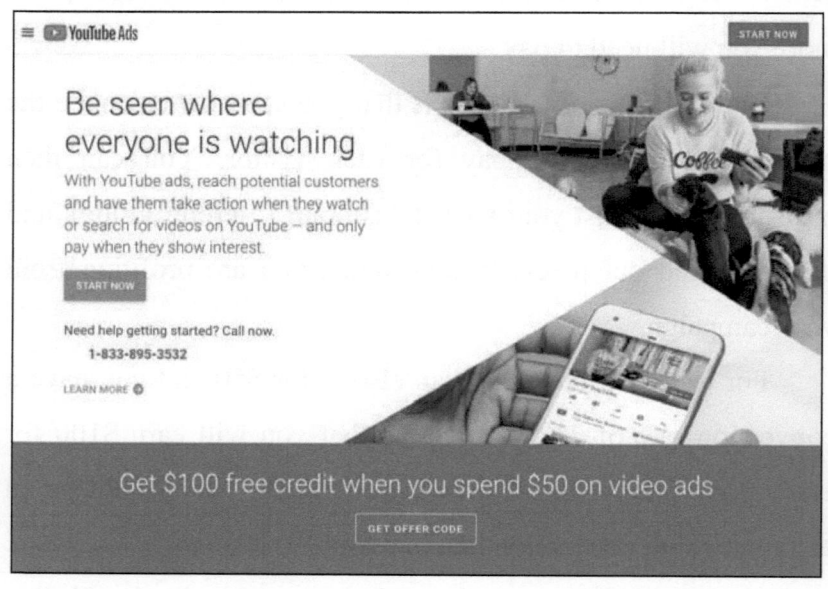

Think about a big influencer like Tai Lopez. Even though he is now being called out for being a "fake guru", he has created popularity by using video ads. The campaign "Here in My Garage" showed before a huge number of videos and was highly memed for being *extremely* transparent. But it also got people talking about Tai, and it led to a huge number of visitors for his real YouTube account.

Imagine the potential impact you could have by using video ads, but combining it with a high energy ad that built up excitement and emotion for your website and your products and services! Of course, we're not saying to be like Tai Lopez, that was just an example of the power of video ads.

CHAPTER 6

BUILDING A BRAND THAT'S MEMORABLE

We have discussed a wide range of different strategies for generating website traffic in this book. We have discussed everything from using traditional SEO to more modern strategies like Schema.org markup language. We've looked at the importance of page optimization, and we've discussed the use of advertising.

But there are countless other strategies for bringing traffic to your website. And one of the big things I want to emphasize before we part ways is that you can promote every single post on your site like you would promote a new product.

That means you should be sharing your content on forums that discuss those topics. It means you should be reaching out to members of the press (especially other big blogs), and it means you should be teasing your audience days prior to its release.

Do everything you can in your power to create "buzz" around every one of your posts, and utilize all the resources you have available to you.

The Importance of a Strong Brand to Bring Everything Together

A big bulk of this book has focused on the importance of delivering value, of offering something new, and of inspiring the audience.

If you can learn to do this, then you will find that your content stands out and that you generate a HUGE amount of traffic over time. This is FAR more effective than attempting to use short-term strategies to gain visitors by spamming the web.

It may take time, but you will stand out, and you will grow. Why is that? Because 99% of brands online just don't care.

I've worked with a whole lot of them. And so often, I see the same thing time and again. A client comes along to order some work, and they show me their website.

Their website doesn't have a brand. The name of their website *is* the keyword (www.getgreatabs.com). They don't believe me when I tell them about the 1% LSI, the keyword density and the organic-looking links.

Rather, they just want that keyword repeated as often as possible. They ask for generic titles for their content:

"Best Diet for Abs" "Top Sit Up Exercises" "How to Lose Belly Fat"

They clearly don't know about the niche they're in, they don't care, and they don't have anything new to say.

And as a result, they fill their site with tired, generic and derivative content that is stuffed with keywords and all tied together with an uninspiring brand. Most of them don't even have a logo and the ones that do either made it themselves in MS Paint, or they paid the lowest amount possible and got something really clichés like a lightbulb or a globe with an arrow moving around it.

Then they tell people to follow them on Facebook where they repeatedly post about 'Check out my new ebook HERE'.

They have nothing interesting or new to say. They've done their research, they know the keywords, and they know that this is a good niche to be in.

But they don't *understand* the niche. They have no heart. And so they are destined for failure.

Worst of all? They have no skill.

Now take a look at the sites you already read on a daily basis. Take a look at your favorite blogs and vlogs. What are they like?

The chances are that they have a clear mission statement and brand. They aren't for everyone, but they have a legion of loyal fans. They have a cool logo, and that logo instantly communicates what their brand is all about and who should listen.

They post content that is interesting and unique. They have a completely different take on the subject, and they write about the highly advanced aspects that most blogs simply don't know about or miss.

They might write about 'Cardio Acceleration for 30% Faster Fat Loss'.

Or they might write about the role of dopamine in encouraging snacking behavior.

In other words, these posts are *interesting* and unique. And they have personality – they're written by the brand owner themselves in a way that is passionate and interesting. It's storytelling.

The site is beautiful and well put together. There's video. There are interactive elements. And the images are crisp and high definition.

In short, it has high production values, and it looks like something that has had time, money and *love* spent on it.

If you want to succeed online – *really succeed* – then that's what you need to build.

How To Create a Memorable Brand

Creating a brand doesn't mean creating a logo. A logo is just one aspect of a brand, and it's not what comes first.

What comes first is a mission statement. A mission statement is a phrase belonging to a business that says what it's all about. This should explain: what, how and why.

What do you make/sell/do?
How do you do it differently?
Why do you do it?

I highly recommend watching Simon Sinek's excellent TED talk on the Golden Circle at this point. It's called *How Great Leaders Inspire Action*.

Most companies will think about the what (we make hats, we design websites, we provide legal advice). Many will think about the how (we use the best materials, we outsource to China, we resell but with a value-add).

But the WHY is what matters most. This is the motivation that spurred you on to get involved in the business in the first place. It is what makes you get out of bed in the morning.

And it's once again why you CANNOT have a successful website/business in a niche or industry that you don't truly care about.

So, if you have a restaurant, maybe your 'why' is because you want to introduce the world to healthier, cleaner and more responsibly sourced food.

If you have a website about fitness, maybe your 'why' is because you want to inspire the feeling of accomplishment in your audience.

Whatever the case, you need to understand this because it is what will give you your value proposition, it is what will give you your design language, and it is what will create your marketing opportunities for you.

This will also allow you to find your 'buyer persona'. This is your ideal customer, and through a combination of surveying and of thinking about your brand, you will be able to draw them up.

Now you need to ensure that your strategy is aimed *at* this person. It is a huge mistake to make a website that you want to be 'for everyone'. If you do that, then it won't be particularly interesting or inspiring to anyone!

The key remember is to make people into real fans. Remember, content marketing and 'new SEO' are about the quality of your followers, not the quantity. You want engagement.

Ask yourself: is yours the kind of brand that someone can be a *fan* of? People don't just know about Apple; they are *fans* of Apple. People are *fans* of Tim Ferriss. They like what these brands stand for; they feel they know them. They want to associate with them.

To get to that point – where your site is inspiring to people – you need to stand for something other than getting clicks on your AdSense.

This is the single most important thing to understand if you're going to succeed on the web. So make sure that you understand your "Why" and that you have an idea of what your audience is looking for. Now make sure that everything from your content, to your social media, to your logo and website design *speak* to these values.

5 POWERFUL
TYPES OF CONTENT

CHAPTER 7

5 POWERFUL TYPES OF CONTENT
TO TRY

YouTube Content

Starting a YouTube channel is something that many brands don't consider. But they do so at their peril.

Because YouTube is the world's leading source of video content, with **83% of consumers** watching content on the platform. For reference, Facebook occupies the number 2 spot with 67%.

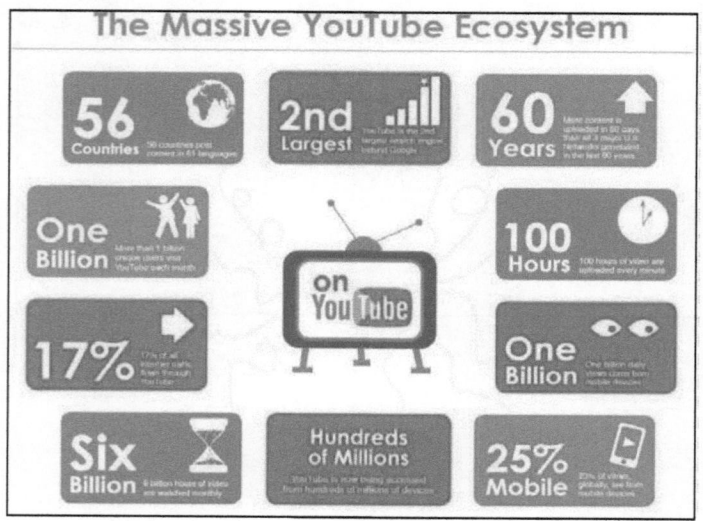

What's more, **7 out of 10 viewers** watch videos to get 'help with a problem' they're experiencing in their job, studies or hobby.

The implication? Producing primarily educational content aimed at resolving your audience's struggles is the way to set yourself up for success.

There are lots of video formats to choose, such as:

- Explainer videos
- Tutorials
- Whiteboard animations
- Interviews
- Talking head
- Vlogs & more

For some inspiration, check out how mediation provider **Headspace** uses their YouTube channel to educate, inspire and entertain their audience.

Their helpful animations and tutorials gently guide viewers and subscribers closer to their brand.

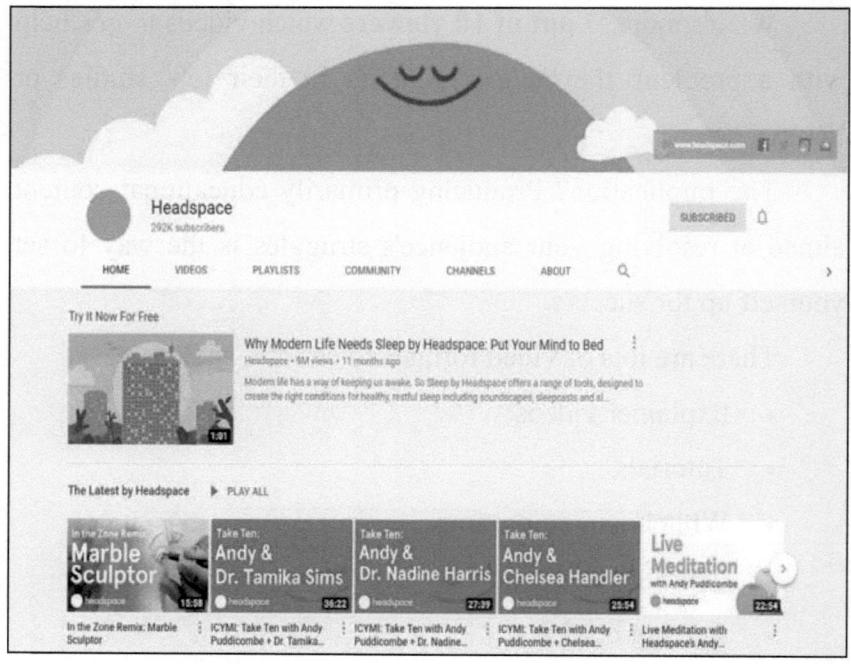

The great thing about creating video content for YouTube is that you can easily repurpose it for other channels.

For example, you can easily take the audio from an interview and turn it into a podcast. Or you can cut video snippets and post them to social media to give your followers micro-nuggets of wisdom.

User-Generated Content

Many brands are overlooking the potential that social offers by skipping over user-generated content. In fact, just a measly **16% of brands** have a documented strategy regarding user-generated content.

And that's a shame because research has shown that UGC pulls in around **28% higher engagement** compared to standard company posts.

What's more, **almost 50% of consumers** say that UGC helps them find new products.

In fact, a recent case study by clothing brand **Burberry attributed a 51%** jump in eCommerce sales year-on-year to the results of their UGC strategy. *Fifty-one-per-cent! Ay caramba!*

The best part about UGC? You don't even have to create it. Your brand advocates do the heavy lifting it for you.

But you do need to encourage them because **over half of consumers** want brands to tell them what type of content to create.

How? It's simple: create a #hashtag campaign.

Just check out how online furniture store Wayfair have created a campaign around the hashtag **#WayfairAtHome** to turn their customers into content creators:

Podcasts

The popularity of podcasts is on the up. In 2018, there **were 48 million weekly podcast listeners**, but by 2021 that's expected to jump to 115 million.

And right now the marketplace is not crazy competitive. There are around 80 million Facebook business pages - but there are only about **750,000 podcasts** airing on a regular basis.

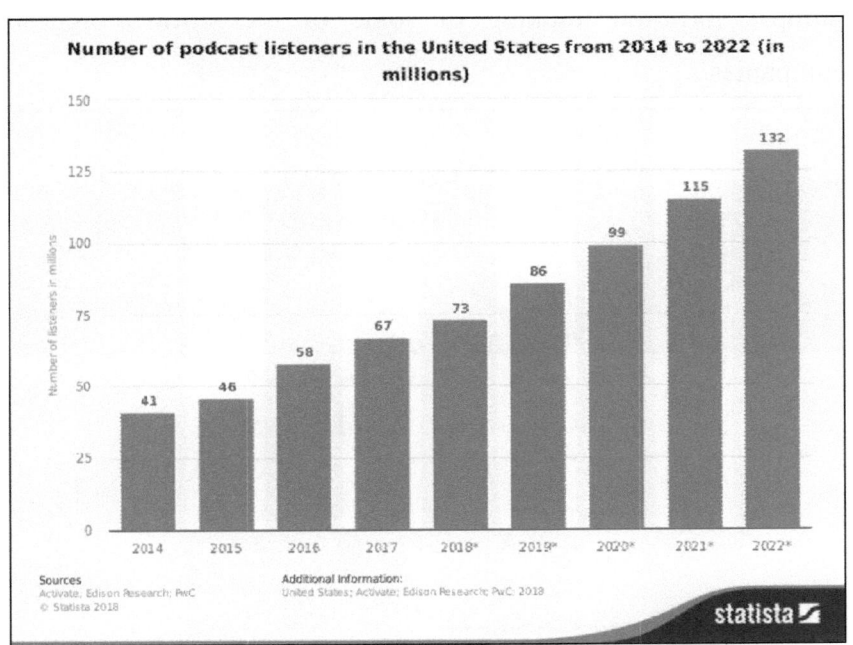

This high demand, coupled with low supply means that now is the perfect time to add podcasting to your content marketing arsenal.

Especially when you consider that the average podcast listener **earns between $10-20k** more than the average US consumer - with 15% of listeners earning $150,000+. Did somebody say higher purchasing power?

For inspiration, check out how Harvard Business Review uses their podcast *'HBR Ideacast'* to give their audience a glimpse into the thinking of some of the world's biggest companies.

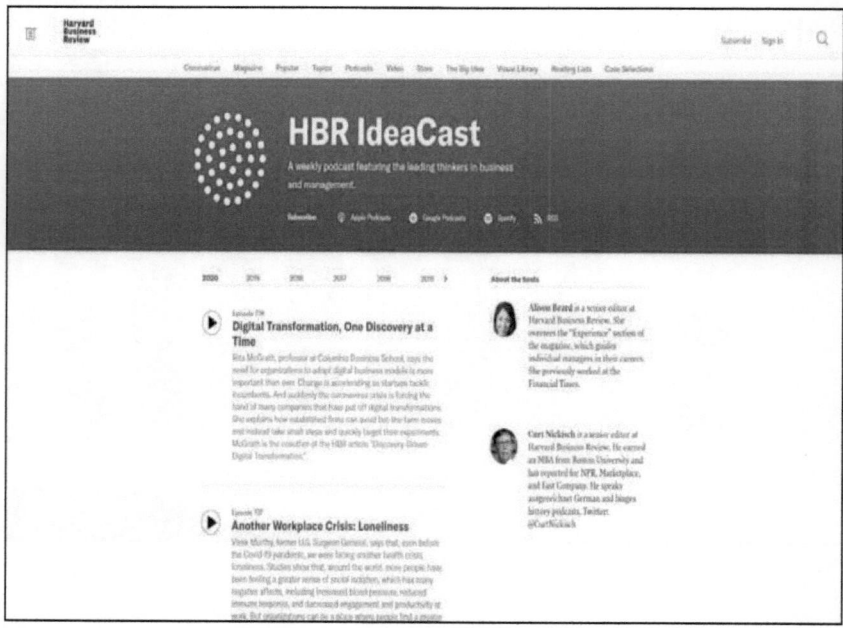

Infographics

Okay, infographics aren't always strictly 'text-free', but they're predominantly a visual medium that you shouldn't overlook.

Why? Well, how about I let an infographic do the talking for me?

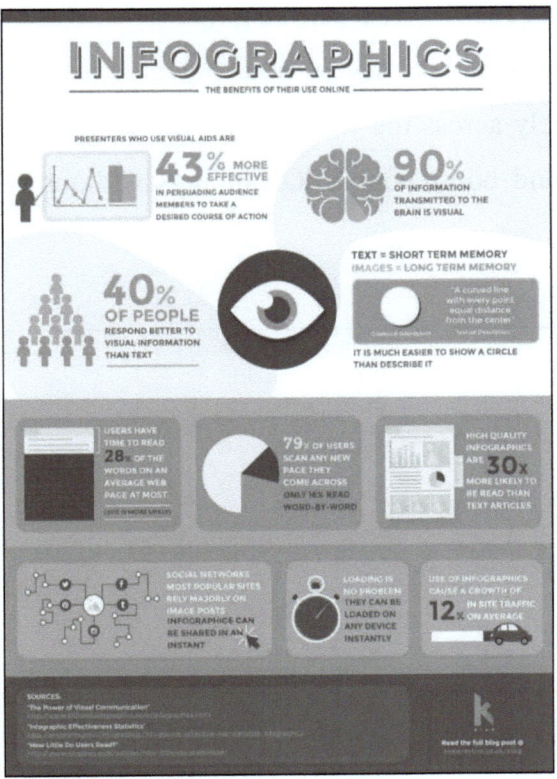

Pretty powerful stuff. As the old adage goes 'a picture is worth a thousand words'.

Infographics appeal to us because they're so easy to consume. The mental effort required to get 'the gold' is so low that we're more likely to retain the message.

In fact, when relevant images are used, eye-tracking studies show readers **spend more time looking at the images than they do reading text on the page.**

Plus infographics have serious potential to go viral - being shared widely across the web they'll help you pick up valuable backlinks and boost your SEO rankings without you lifting a finger.

You might be thinking, that's great - but I can't afford to hire a graphic designer right now. Don't worry, you don't have to.

You can use a tool like **Pictochart** to create beautiful infographics with a simple drag and drop editor. Who says life needs to be complicated?

Courses

Developing educational courses is an incredibly powerful content marketing tactic.

Courses are especially potent if you're selling higher-priced services or software, but they can still be useful for physical products too.

Sharing your professional experience with your audience creates a strong sense of reciprocity and showcases your expertise.

Take software company **HPLife,** for example. They offer business and start-up courses for free, with some of HP's products at the heart of each lesson.

They've improved how hundreds of thousands of entrepreneurs run their business, but better yet, they've indirectly trained those people to use their products and services.

Obviously creating a course of your own doesn't have to involve the level of effort HP have put into their Life academy.

You can use a platform like **Teachable** (or YouTube is always good) to create free short courses. Or even just run a once-off webinar focused on educating your audience.

You'll find that once you start giving value like this, you'll get it back in spades.

CHAPTER 8

CONCLUSION

Hopefully, by now, you're equipped with the tips and strategies for generating traffic to your website and building your following online.

There're endless opportunities to drive traffic, generate awareness, build relationships and bring in revenue.

One small word of caution: don't try to jump in and do multiple things at once. Spreading yourself too thinly isn't going do you any favors.

Instead, pick one to two mediums and go all-in on it for the best chance of success.

Printed by Libri Plureos GmbH in Hamburg, Germany